To my friend Harold C. Case
And to my beloved congregation at Daniel L. Marsh Chapel,
Boston University

Temptations of Jesus

by Howard Thurman

Five Sermons given in Marsh Chapel
Boston University, 1962

Friends United Press
Richmond, Indiana

Printed in the United States of America
Published by Friends United Press
101 Quaker Hill Drive
Richmond, IN 47374

Published by arrangement with the author.
Lawton Kennedy edition published 1962.

Friends United Press edition published 1978.

Fourth Printing 1995
Fifth Printing 1997

Foreword

Here are five sermons preached in Marsh Chapel during the month of July, in the year of our Lord, 1962. They are a faithful transcription of the spoken word from tape recordings made for rebroadcasting to a radio audience in the evening of the Sunday on which each was delivered. The minimum of editing has been done in order that the clarity of expression might be maintained despite the change of the medium from the spoken to the written word.

These are five sermons on certain dilemmas of Jesus, growing out of temptations which he faced. They are not five lectures. They are not five critical essays. They are five sermons, having as their fundamental purpose the illumination of the imagination, the stirring of the heart, and the challenge to live life meaningfully.

We see the Master as he struggled to find a way which will be for him The Way in which he can walk in utter harmony with the Will of his Father and the purpose of life. This too is what we seek, and in his answer we may find precious clues for ourselves. He was tempted as all men are tempted and his example leaves the whole world in his debt.

The publishing of this little book in a special, limited first edition, designed and printed by Lawton Kennedy of San Francisco, is the fulfillment of a long cherished dream which we have had for many years, since this artist-publisher began printing the annual Christmas and other special occasion cards which I have written for the Church for the Fellowship of All Peoples in San Francisco, and later for Marsh Chapel in Boston. With customary grace, Eugene Exman, of Harper and Brothers, has granted me temporary release from my contract in order to make possible a unique Lawton Kennedy production.

It so happens that this was the last sermon-series which I presented in Marsh Chapel, marking the end of a nine-year period of active responsibility for that part of the religious life of Boston University, as expressed in the preaching and ministry of Marsh Chapel, and the beginning of a two-year leave for an extended ministry in the service of the University, to other areas of the United States and countries abroad.

The material presented here was later used as the basis of the Theme Devotional Addresses at the meeting of the 20th General Council of the United Church of Canada, including the Congregational, Methodist, and Presbyterian denominations, held at the Metropolitan United Church, London, Ontario, September twelfth through the nineteenth. Significantly, the addresses delivered before this inspiring body marked the first major assignment in the wider ministry of the next two years.   HOWARD THURMAN

Boston University
September, 1962

ACKNOWLEDGMENTS

Appreciation is given for permission to use the following quotations: "The Brothers," "The Rich Young Ruler," and "Martha of Bethany" from *The Witnesses and Other Poems* by Clive Sansom published by Methuen & Co., Ltd., London; selections from *From Man to Man* by Olive Schreiner published by Harper & Row, Inc., New York; and from *The Choir Invisible* by James Lane Allen published by The Macmillan Company, New York.

Table of Contents

Not by Bread—Alone

Meditation:

We bring into the quietness of Thy Presence, our Father, all the particulars of our lives. We would not hold back from Thy scrutiny any facet of ourselves:

The things of which we are ashamed and by which our spirits are embarrassed; the good things which we have done and the good impulses of which we are aware; those whom we recognize by ties of kinship, but with whom we have no fellowship; those whom we recognize by ties of kinship and with whom we have deep and abiding fellowship; those whom we love as best we can; those whom we have not yet learned how to want to love; the quiet satisfaction of some part of us that is found in the strength of hostility and the reinforcement of bitterness of heart.

Our maladies we bring before Thee: The things in our bodies that have given us trouble, which we cannot quite shake off despite all of the skill of the minds of men and all the wisdom of the art of healing; those deep and turbulent upheavals in our spirits that keep our minds divided and our emotions in revolt.

Into the quietness, our Father, we bring all the facets of our lives; we hold them there, trying to restrain ourselves lest we ask of Thee that which is not in accordance with Thy Purpose and Thy Will; waiting that we may discern the movement of Thy Spirit amidst all the hinterland of our region.

Of all the peoples of the world and of all the troubled places, we bring only one before Thee this morning—the turbulent, pain-wracked, suffering spirit of Algeria. After more than a hundred leaden-footed days and months and years, our Father, this day they will speak with freedom what it is in their hearts to say as Thy

[13]

children. Brood over that troubled land to the end that some way may be found for the great healing, for forgiveness of Frenchmen and Moslem.

O God, do not despair of us. Do not despair of us, but hold us with Thy Love until we learn how to love.

O God, do not despair of us, our Father. . . .

Temptations of Jesus

I begin this morning a journey which we shall be taking having to do with certain of the fundamental dilemmas in the life of the Master.

As a background for our consideration today I want to read two things, one by Oscar Wilde *(De Profundis)*, and the other by the British poet, Clive Sansom *(The Witnesses and Other Poems)*.

"There is still something to me almost incredible in the idea of a young Galilean peasant imagining that he could bear on his own shoulders the burden of the entire world: all that had already been done and suffered, and all that was yet to be done and suffered: the sins of Nero, of Caesar Borgia, of Alexander the Sixth, and of him who was Emperor of Rome and Priest of the Sun: the sufferings of those whose names are legion and whose dwelling is among the tombs: oppressed nationalities, factory children, thieves, people in prison, outcasts, those who are dumb under oppression and whose silence is heard only of God; and not merely imagining this but actually achieving it, so that at the present moment all who come in contact with his personality, even though they may neither bow to his altar or kneel before his priest, in some way find that the ugliness of their sin is taken away and the beauty of their sorrow revealed to them."

In this, from the British poet, "The Brothers" address Jesus:

Going from Nazareth? Where? —To the Jordan valley?
Leaving your home and your trade, your own kinsfolk?
For what? For an unwashed preacher, a ranting hermit
Who sacrificed family and wealth, and a seat in the priesthood
For locusts and prophecies? Why—you are mad, insane,
Selling your life for a whim, a religious frenzy.
Mad, yes, mad. Will you share his faith and his filth,
Outcasts like him, rejected by brother and friend,
A life of rebellion, hunger, a shameful death?

If the thought of that leaves you unmoved, then remember us
Your brothers and sisters, the mother who gave you birth.
See her there, standing in tears, forsaken, bewildered,
Left by her first-born, you, the head of the household.
Think of her neighbours' looks, the humiliation,
Her fears and her griefs. What? What do you say?
'Whoever obeys the will of my father in heaven
Is my brother, my sister, my mother.'—By the God of Israel!
Would you preach at us? —your ministry start at home?

Better recall, if you can, your father in Nazareth,
Your pledge to him, your promise of filial care.
'You shall honour your father and mother,' Remember that
When you mouth your texts. Remember that:
And carry for ever the shame of your father's children.

It is very important to lay a general foundation for our thinking together about certain of the dilemmas of Jesus. A dilemma is the kind of problem that a man faces when live options, alternatives, are presented to him, any one of which is not quite a satisfying solution to the problem that confronts him. Very often when we are faced with our dilemmas, we are not as fortunate as is indicated by a sign I saw thirty years ago at a town in Texas called Big Sandy. My train coach stopped across a highway; I looked out of the window and saw a huge sign. It must have been twenty feet high and about twenty feet square. It read: "FIVE HIGHWAYS MEET HERE. FOUR CHANCES TO GO WRONG. ASK US." But we aren't as fortunate as that when we face our dilemmas.

Jesus of Nazareth had what seems to me to have been a fundamental and searching—almost devastating—experience of God. This experience was so fontal and so fundamental to the very grounds of his being that he had to deal with the implications of this experience whenever he raised any question about the meaning and function of his own life. When he heard that John the Baptist was preaching at the Jordan River, it must have been quite a problem for him.

—Shall I go and hear him or shall I ignore him? If my personal and private and intimate religious experience, my experience of God is valid, if it is authentic, if it is dependable, then I do not need any other-than-self reference. And besides, John is saying to everybody, 'Repent of your sins and receive the Kingdom of God.' What does this say to me if I go down there and present myself for baptism? If I accept baptism at his hands, then doesn't this give to his utterances and his movements the sanction of my heart and my mind, as if what he is saying and what he is doing represent the fulfillment of the meaning of that which I, myself, have experienced under God?

This is always the dilemma. Shall I wait until the most perfect thing comes along and identify myself with that, or shall I accept something that doesn't quite say all that I think can be said, but is the best that is being said at this particular time?

We feel this way sometimes about the church, don't we? We forget that the church is made up of the halt and the lame and the blind; the sinners, the prejudiced, those whose hearts are bitter and those whose hearts are sweet. It is made up of the people who make up the world. I knew a man in Oberlin, when I was the minister there, who would not join my church, or any church, because he said that he did not want to lose his soul. He said that as long as he stayed out of the church, he could be greatly exercised about trying to follow Jesus, but if he joined the church, he would become confused. There are many people who feel that way. Well, Jesus may have felt that way about John. But at any rate, he presented himself for baptism.

When Jesus was baptised of John, a very extraordinary thing happened to him. It seemed to him that the heavens opened and that the living Spirit of the living God descended upon him like a dove and in the midst of this experience, he heard a Voice . . . and the Voice said, "You are my Son, in whom I am well pleased."

And then he left; shaken to his core.

— I must find some place of complete and utter isolation, a chance to sense the bearings of this tremendous experience, lest I find myself betraying it or betrayed by it.

He went into the wasteland. To sit it out. To think. To weigh and to wait.

There is a Congregational Church in Chicago, about ten blocks from the Loop, where there is an amazing painting of The Temptations of Jesus. Jesus is seated on a rock overlooking a valley. That much is the traditional image which artists portray. He is looking straight ahead. As you stand watching the figure, your eyes get adjusted to the light on it, and this is what you see—dozens of fingers clutching at his mind.

— What shall I do with my life if I am going to be true to the tremendous experience of God which I have had? How can I live so that my life will not deny the glory which I saw and felt? Or was the glory which I saw and felt completely other-worldly and beyond any thing that human experience can seek to implement? Is it something that is separate and is not to be a part of the warp and woof, the stuff of human experience? Was I invaded by something that does not belong to the nature and the character of the normal working paper of human life? This is the question.

And then, after a long time thinking, pro-ing and con-ing, if-ing, but-on-the-other-hand-ing, his eyes fell on a stone at his feet and the stone looked just like one of the cakes that his mother used to make. At once he became aware of something which had been on the periphery of his mind for a long time; but he hadn't gotten around to it. It hadn't moved to the center of his consciousness. He was hungry. And then the struggle was on.

— If it is true that you are the Son of God, *you are* the Son of God, the *Son of God*, then the moment coming up out of the water of the River Jordan, when the heavens opened and you could scarcely discern between that which was you and that which was the Light, the Shekinah of your Father—

this moment was The Moment of all your life. So! Why not reduce that moment to a manageable unit of confirmation by putting it to work to administer to the needs which must be met in you, if you are to be released to be in the world what you can be. Turn the stones to bread.

Thus argued the Tempter.

For a long time, all he could think of were these few words, 'Man, man must not live by bread . . .'

—But there is something wrong with that. Man has to have bread. Man must not live by bread. . . . Man must not live by bread. . . . bread. . . . by bread—but men *do* live by bread. And if a man is hungry, he can't get through to his spirit unless, unless his hunger has been selected as the avenue through which he seeks the highway of God. But if the hunger is another kind, you can't get through to him until you meet the hunger. Man *does* live by bread. But man does. . . . but man. . . . but bread. . . . If I have all the bread I need, and something else doesn't happen, I am still a poor. . . . There is something wrong with this. Man. . . . Man does not live by bread ALONE!

It must have been days between the first part of the sentence and the last word. I wonder how many weary hours he said it over and over again—Man must not live by bread—not being able to get beyond it, until at last, there must have leaped into his mind, like a flash of blinding light, one word: *Alone*. Ah! This is a practical world even for one who has seen visions and who feels that there is incumbent upon him some peculiar ministry to his people, or to other people. Nevertheless, even for him, it is a practical world. "Man must not live by bread alone, but by every word that proceedeth out of the mouth of God."

Man must get bread to eat. He must organize the resources of his life in an effort to build some kind of windbreak against the impersonal operation of the economic and social order by which he is surrounded, so that with some measure of balance and equilibrium and tranquility he might reproduce his kind and preserve some seed against the impersonal workings of the future. This is a necessity for man. He must be a bread-winner. He must wrest from the stubborn and recalcitrant and unyielding earth the stuff that he needs to build his body and to bring assurance and health and well-being to his children. Man must do this. But the *bias*, the emphasis, the prejudice, the slant of his life must be on the side of the hungers of his mind and his spirit. Do you believe that?

It is easy to believe it when you are not hungry. There is an old Zulu proverb that says, "Full-belly child says to empty-belly child, 'Be of good cheer.' Only the empty-belly child has the right to say to the empty-belly child, 'Be of good cheer'."

Do you believe that the bias, the loaded energy of your life must always be on the side of those things that are addressed to the deepest and most searching hungers of your mind and your spirit? And if, in the swing of your years, you must make the choice, how will you vote? For where your treasure is, there your life will be. How does our society vote on this? How does the church vote on this? How do you vote? How do you vote? How?

Forgive us for our sins, our Father; leave us not to the weakness of our strength, or to the strength of our weakness, but tutor us in Thy graces that we may not deny in the darkness, the light which we have seen at other times. And for us, this is enough.

Amen.

Tempt God?

Meditation:

Our Father, we would bring before Thee, as we offer our prayer, the far-flung needs of Thy children everywhere. Some of the needs we recognize as part and parcel of the full or limited measure of our own responsibilities. Some of the needs seem far removed from where we are, and they but underscore the littleness and impotency of our own lives. We would share all of this, you see, our Father, but our minds and our hearts are caught and held by our own private predicament and our own great personal need. So wilt Thou understand us and deal gently with us as we speak to Thee about the concerns of our hearts out of the private life with which we are so utterly familiar.

We are mindful that we are sinners and when we say this, our Father, we are not thinking of ways by which we have not conformed to some great external law, or doctrine, or theology, but when we say that we are sinners, our Father, we are talking very personally to Thee about our own experiences of our own limitations—all the mean things to which we have yielded, either in moments of weakness or of pride; the bad thoughts that we have had even as our faces were smiling and our eyes were glowing; the things that we have refrained from doing when we felt the urge to do them, because they were right and decent; whole and clean. These are the things, our Father, that we mean as we talk to Thee about our sins. Wilt Thou forgive us that we may try again where we have failed before?

Our fears, our Father, are very present and we know that this is no place, before Thee in all the quietness, to talk of the tempest and the torture of our private fears, but they are a part of our lives:

Fear of sickness and bodily failure, fear of desertion and loneliness, fear of our jobs, fear of the instability of our own economic lives, fear for our families and our children, fear of life itself. And it is so wonderful, our Father, that as we talk with Thee about this, the fears are not always present; there are moments when we are free. Our very spirits take wings and all the things that imprison and hold, like the fears and anxieties, are left behind and we look down upon them from afar and wonder why they could hold such sway over our lives. There are these moments that come to us, and we thank Thee for them. May we remember them when the fears close in upon us!

Our dreams are before us and before Thee, our Father; the dreams which we have forgotten until in the quietness, all the stillness before Thee brings them back with their living touch — there are things that we had planned for our lives at some earlier time, the way we thought the future would unfold for us, and somewhere along the way something happened to us and the dream faded — maybe a wrong turn in the road, we don't know; but as we sit together in the quietness, fingering the dreams of our lives, our hearts yearn for a fulfillment which has never been ours.

O God, Keeper of the dreams of Thy children, leave us not alone. Leave us not alone, but be in us and about us even as Thy Spirit doth surround us, to the end that we may take courage, without which, our Father, our very spirits sicken and die.

O God who will not let us go, teach us how to hold fast to Thee, our Father.

> "If Thou but suffer God to guide thee
> And hope in Him thro' all the ways,
> He'll give thee strength, whate'er betide thee,
> And bear thee thro' the evil days;
> Who trusts in God's unchanging love
> Builds on the rock that naught can move."

Temptations of Jesus

We are continuing our thinking together about certain of the dilemmas of Jesus, and today we consider *another* aspect of the dilemma in the wilderness. First, I want to read two things by the same British poet from whom I read last week.

THE RICH YOUNG RULER

'What must I do, master, to gain
Eternal life?
From my youth I have kept the Commandments,
Honoured my parents;
Theft, murder, lying, adultery —
All these
By God's mercy have passed me by.
What then must I do, master?
What more must I do?'
'Sell all,' he replied, 'And follow me.'
An easy saying.
He, a carpenter, a carpenter's son,
Sacrificed nothing.
And his man Peter — smirking, self-righteous —
What did he lose
But some worn nets, a boat-share,
And trade in the market?
It wasn't myself I was thinking of —
Ease and possessions —
But the responsibility of wealth
Towards its dependents.
What of them, if I had obeyed him —
What of my servants?
That's what I tell myself, now —

But do I believe it?
Then—silent—I walked away,
Watching my sandals,
While his voice, the voice of my heart,
Followed me homeward.
In misery, I stopped by the lake.
Hid by the crowd-wall,
I heard him speak of the Kingdom of God,
The camel, the needle.

MARTHA OF BETHANY

It's all very well
Sitting in the shade of the courtyard
Talking about your souls.
Someone's got to see to the cooking,
Standing at the oven all morning
With you two taking your ease.
It's all very well
Saying he'd be content
With bread and honey.
Perhaps he would—but I wouldn't,
Coming to our house like this,
Not giving him of our best.
Yes, it's all very well
Him trying to excuse you,
Saying your recipe's best,
Saying I worry too much,
That I'm always anxious.
Someone's got to worry—
And double if the others don't care.
For it's all very well
Talking of faith and belief,
But what would you do
If everyone sat in the cool
Not getting their meals?
And he can't go wandering and preaching

On an empty stomach—
He'd die in the first fortnight.
Then where would you be
With all your discussions and questions
And no one to answer them?
It's all very well.

And then these few sentences by James Lane Allen *The Choir Invisible:*

"To see justice go down and not believe in the triumph of injustice; for every wrong that you weakly deal another or another deals you to love more and more the fairness and beauty of what is right; and so to turn with ever-increasing love from the imperfection that is in us all to the Perfection that is above us all—the perfection that is God."

The Tempter took him to the pinnacle of the Temple and he said to him,

—If you are the Son of God, jump down from the pinnacle and it will be all right. Nothing will happen to you. Why? Because you are someone very special and God will give his angels charge concerning you, as the Psalmist says, and upon their wings they will bear your feet lest you hurt yourself in some way.

And the Master replied,

—Man must not tempt God, even a good man.

What is the essence of the dilemma? You have thought of it many times and it is all so familiar that anything I say to you this morning you may have heard before, but nevertheless I am going to say it.

The Tempter said to him that this world is not orderly. It is not structured. There is no fundamental dependability upon which the individual living expression of life may depend. But if you can manage to get into a certain position of immunity, then the ordinary logic of life can be handled and manipulated.

The implication of the Master's reply to the Tempter is this:

—If I go up to the pinnacle of the Temple and jump down, the possibilities are I will break my neck, Son of God to the contrary notwithstanding, because this is an orderly world and if I act as though I am immune to the logic, the logic itself will destroy me.

Do you believe that?

Life is rooted and grounded in a structure of dependability. It is this that makes it possible for the private enterprise, or the collective enterprise, to be sustained by life. If I ignore this fact, then the very force of life itself becomes an instrument of death in my hands. Let's see what this means in terms of the intimate dilemma which Jesus faced.

We experience it in our own time. The mind of man has been activating its affinity with the external world of nature, and as a result, man has been able to lift out of the world of nature many things which are inherent in its order. As man has lifted these things out and observed them and reduced them to manageable units of control and manipulation, he has made the order of nature become an instrument in his hands for the fulfillment of private ends, ends which themselves may be destructive of the very nature that gave the secret in the first place. And that means, in simple terms, that when the secret of atomic energy becomes available to man and man uses this knowledge, skill, power, and insight for ends that are exclusive of his fellows, in other words, when he uses it in ways that will give him a kind of immunity against the moral quality of human relations, then the very order itself, the very logic itself, the very energy of the atom itself becomes the stalking manifestation of the *wrath* of God. But if he uses the knowledge for ends that are inclusive of his fellows and their needs, the very energy itself becomes a manifestation of the *love* of God. When man experiences that kind of community, achievements of health and meaning and vitality and fulfillment become available unlike anything that had harassed or haunted his mind through all the generations of the past.

One other word in this connection. There is something even more personal here, it seems to me. It is reasonable for a man to say: If I am good, if I try to do the best I can, if I have followed the law of my heart, and in ways that were deliberate and conscious, tried to understand the will of God and put myself at its disposal, if I have not withheld my compassion from the needy, and have offered my thanksgiving to God for all of the manifestations of graces by which he has surrounded and sustained my life, if I have an inner sense of harmony and peace with His Spirit—then this ought to give me certain pragmatic advantages in life. I ought to be privileged to be an exception to the rules that bind people who have not been acting this way. Have you ever felt that way? Consider something you yourself are experiencing, and then look across the street and see a person who, from your point of view, has violated everything that you regard as holy and sacred. Yet—what he touches seems to blossom, and what you touch seems to wither and die as soon as it looks in your face. It's peculiar. You have felt that way!

Jesus may have thought:

—Somehow the quality of my character ought to render me immune to the order of life. Life should make an exception in my case because I am Jesus! Because of that great moment when I felt the affirmation and the confirmation of my Father! —When he gave to me the complete and utter sanction and imprimatur of His whole Being—under the aegis and sweep of that sense of glory and communion and identity—I seemed to have been lifted out of all the categories by which men are bound and held. Why can't I, then, act with utter disregard for all of this?

A friend of mine who is a doctor, was the dean of a medical school once upon a time. Many years ago I went to him for a physical examination. I was making a change in my plan of life and I wanted to know what was working for me and what would be working against me. He gave me his part of the exam and then sent me to about five other people to do various things. At the end of about a week I got a telephone call from him telling me that he wanted to see me. You know the sense of destiny that rides on that. You walk into his office; you sit in the chair and he sits at his desk. He has a manila folder and in it there are sheets of paper with typing and graphs and a lot of things you don't understand. He opens the folder, looks at you and says, "Hmmm, hmmm. . . . Uhmmm." Then he hesitates on one page, looks at you again, and then, it is a great relief, he turns it over and says, "Hmmm." And so he goes, all the way through. Well, that's what my doctor did, and I rejoiced to see him close the folder. I knew that I had made it. Then he said to me, "You are in fine shape. Your heart, your lungs, all those things are in good order, but you are too heavy."

He talked with me rather learnedly about what the extra pounds I was carrying would do to my heart and lungs and bloodvessels—all kinds of things that were very frightening to me. Then I looked at him! He wasn't as tall as I, and he weighed about two hundred and twenty-five pounds. *He thought that his body knew that he was a doctor.* His body did not know that he was a doctor; his body knew precisely what my body knew. We were bound by the same relentless logic of orderedness that provides the structure of dependability for life. Because he knew something about the structure had no bearing on this fact. It gave him no immunity, unless his knowledge enabled him to operate more fully, more effectively, more creatively *within* the order than my lack of knowledge.

This is a part of the dilemma of the trained mind, isn't it? Because we are trained, because we know so much about some things, in very subtle ways this counsels us into a kind of delusion about the extent to which we ourselves are just a part of the ebb and flow and order of life. Unless the knowledge gives us insight that will enable us to function in ways that will use the structure of dependability as a resource for the highest fulfillment in life, then the very knowledge that we have tempts us to put ourselves against life. And very quietly, without blasting of trumpets, without making any noise, life just grinds us to powder.

This is what the Master saw.

With all the embodiment which I feel of the very living Spirit of God, with all the "for instances" of His Kingdom, and the Angelos of His Spirit that has as its fundamental purpose the renewing and the regenerating of life so that more and more, all of life will come under the sweep of the gentle approval of the Will and Mind of the Love of God; nevertheless, I still must operate within the structure that *holds*. When I get out of it, life becomes the Enemy. When I am in it, life becomes the Resource. When I get out of it I experience the Wrath of God. When I am within it I experience the Love of God.

And the Tempter carried him to the pinnacle of the Temple and said,

—It is all right for you to jump. God will guarantee you.

If the dilemma were real, if the temptation were real, Jesus could have failed. If he could not have failed, there is no meaning in his freedom. I am so very glad that he struggled and triumphed. And so he speaks to me all the time that I might struggle, if, happily, I too might triumph. But if I felt that when the pressure was upon him, he had an out, then when the pressure is upon me I could not hear him speak to me. Because he triumphed, there is laid upon my soul a necessity that I can never shake, that there is a way. There is a way.

Leave us not, our Father, to the strength of our weakness or the weakness of our strength. Hold us, O God, hold us until at last there begins to move deep within us the response to Thy Love. This is what we want, O God, so much, so very, very much, our Father.

Amen.

The Kingdoms of this World

Meditation:

"A curse on him who relies on man, and leans upon mere human aid, turning his thoughts from the Eternal! He is like some desert scrub that never thrives, set in a dry place in the steppes, in a salt, solitary land. But happy he who relies on the Eternal, with the Eternal for his confidence! He is like a tree planted beside a stream, reaching its roots to the water; untouched by any fear of scorching heat, its leaves are ever green, it goes on bearing fruit in days of drought."

It is so easy, our Father, for us to say those words, and even in the saying of them there are moments when we sense our identity with them, but the conflict in our spirits goes so deep. There is something reassuring and confident and visible about the strength, the presence, the activity of man, something we can understand and touch, something that is flesh of our flesh and bone of our bone, and mind of our mind. There is something so mysterious and sometimes distant, our Father, when we use words about Thee. They seem either empty, or so full of meaning that we are devastated and made desolate by the barrenness of our own lives in contrast. But beneath the conflict, beneath the churning turmoil and turbulence, we sense something more, if we could just hold it against all that divides and separates, in weakness and in strength, in sin and in righteousness, if we could hold it against the despair of our spirits or against the soaring height of our dreams!

O God, we do want to know Thy Presence, to feel the movement of Thy Spirit at our depths. We do hunger for the cleansing of Thy Grace. Wilt Thou take unto Thyself our hearts desiring and wilt Thou follow along all its courses, until at last we are in Thee and Thou art in us. Above all else this speaks to our condition O God, God, God . . .

[35]

Temptations of Jesus

As a background for our consideration of the third leg in our journey on certain dilemmas of Jesus, I am reading two things. First, from *The Inward Journey:*

He had wondered about the hill above the rock on which he sat.
In and out of his mind the query came.
A little while before the sun was lost beyond the hill
He stirred himself to move.
At the top of the hill he stood transfixed:
    The sun nestled on the edge of a cloud at bay—
    A soft iridescence blanketed all the air above, below.

To the East the clouds were alive with many forms:
        Chariots, horsemen, and marching legions,
        Men and women in ceaseless motion
        Filling a thousand market squares with mild commotion.
And high above, disappearing in the heavens
Huge columns resting on the vast panorama
As on a living throne:
        The kingdoms of this world—

        Jesus looked and trembled.

Darkness crept down; the stars returned.
Slowly he started back along the path.
The kingdoms of this world . . .
"What if I could . . . Oh, No!
Suppose I could. It is too fantastic.
If I could bring it off:
All their force and power
An instrument for good.
By mighty acts which none could brook
Fear and hunger would disappear.

[37]

The deeds of peace would banish plans for war.
Such is my Father's will.
But how could these things be?
If all the God in me could serve the world,
Kings, kingdoms, earthly rulers all
Would disappear.
And in their place the Mind of God would sit enthroned.
His son would rule for Him.
The praise due Him and Him alone would come to me . . .

    I heard the Voice, His Voice."

        Thou shalt worship God alone
        And Him only shalt thou serve.

And then this written by an anonymous poet.

        Two statesmen met by midnight.
        Their ease was partly feigned,
        They glanced about the prairie,
        Their faces were constrained.
        In various ways aforetime
        They had misled the state,
        Yet did it so politely
        Their henchmen thought them great.
        They sat beneath a hedge and spoke
        No word, but had a smoke.
        A satchel passed from hand to hand—
        Next day the deadlock broke.

We talked last Sunday about the dilemma that was created for
Jesus, and is created for any man, by the great delusion that because
of some special set of extenuating circumstances, life will make an
exception in his case, because he is different.

Today, we are considering the dilemmas created by a very deep
and searching sense of commitment which Jesus had to the Kingdom of God. And even more than a commitment to the Kingdom

of God, a deep sense of the way life had unfolded *in* him, particularly, since the moment of high and staggering illumination at the baptism. He was thinking of himself, more and more, as the living embodiment of the Kingdom of God, the "for instance" of the Kingdom. The one thing that he wanted to do as the result of this deep inner sense of involvement in the Will of his Father was to be able, by the details of his living, by the procedures by which he structured his private enterprise, to bring the kingdoms of this world under the rule and the order and control of God.

The Tempter may have said to him:

—I know this is what you want to do. And you can do it. You have vision. You have youth. You have a sense of the living Presence of the Living God. Everything is on your side for doing it, because you are It already! But there is a little formality here. The kingdoms of this world belong to me. They are mine. Now, you know that God made you. God made mankind. It is true that God created the world of nature, time and space, and all the interlocking ingredients that give to our experiences a sense of context, but He did not make the relationships that exist between man and man, between man and nature. *I* made those. *I* made them. If you want to change the order, you must change the relationships and you cannot change the relationships unless you reduce me to zero.

This is very interesting. The relationships that exist between the things that God created are not created by God.

Many years ago when I was a student in Rochester, New York, I went into a haberdashery to get a pair of shoes. It was one of those famous Rochester days. The sun hadn't been around for a long time; it was wet and slushy; snowy and icy—just one of those days when the weather seems quite personal.

The salesman asked, "What size shoe do you wear?"

I replied, "Ten."

"What kind?"

"Black oxfords."

He went out, came back with a box, and then suddenly turned around and carried the box out. He returned, took off my shoe, measured my foot, went out again and brought back another pair of shoes. I put them on. They fit and I paid him. I wasn't anxious to get right out into that weather again and tarried for a while. I was the only customer in the store and the salesman said to me, "You know, this is an awful job that I have."

"Oh," I said, "It seems pretty good to me. You walk around all dressed up, and you wear a boutonniere and you don't have to work hard."

But he replied, "Oh, I don't mean that. You see, I get tired lying."

"Lying?" I asked.

"Yes. We are not supposed to let the customer know the size of his feet. When the sun is shining and it is a beautiful day, it doesn't worry me very much. But when the weather is heavy, then my conscience stirs and I don't like it. I decide that I am going to do something about it, but then I remember this is a very good job and it pays enough, and I see the face of my little boy, and my wife, and I smile and just go on."

"Well," I said, "You won't have to worry about my telling the manager that you told me the truth. What size *did* you sell me?"

"Twelve," he said.

The context in which destiny has to be worked out, in which the person who is committed to the Kingdom of God must fulfill his commitment, is a context that again and again is not responsive to the individual's will, however good and high and holy that will may be. The kingdoms of this world spring out of one of the most fundamental and persistent aspects of personality—the need for power, power to be able to bring the world of nature under subjection so that it can become the instrument of human desire; power over time and space so that wherever I will to be, with reference to any arrangement of details, will be under the control of my mind and my desire; power over the lives of other human beings. These are the powers that the kingdoms of this world represent. The state, as the state, is able to provide reasonable security for its citizens. It is able to address itself and its will to the private personal needs of individual citizens so that they will not suffer from the ravages of hunger or be exposed to the unrestrained violence of their fellows. In relation to the individual, the state stands as the controller of power—power over nature, power over time and space, and power over the lives of the individuals who make up the state.

A scheme of affairs is built upon power and is organized so as to keep the controls concentrated in order that progress might take place, and that human life might be sustained. When an individual feels that a state is demanding of him the deep inner nerve center of his consent, and that if he gives it, he relinquishes his right to live and work on behalf of the ideals and dreams that spring out of what to him is a deeper and more searching loyalty, then he faces the problem that Jesus faced.

—Here is Rome, organized, powerful, established. It is in control of my people, Israel. We have lost our political rights; we do not have any kind of authentic political autonomy. The structure of our inner organization does not even permit us to execute a judgment which we may pass in accordance with our inner laws. We are an under-privileged minority in this vast Greco-Roman world. Any person who acts in his private thoughts, judgments and convictions, as if he will hold out against the will of the Empire is a threat to the Empire and its power rests on its ability to absorb all threats. What is the role for someone who feels about the Kingdom of God, the Rule of God, as I feel? What is my role in the state? Shall I go along with it? Now it just may be that if I play the thing right, I will get into a strategic position with the state; once in that position, I will be able to do all the things that are in my heart to do for God, but I can't do anything if I don't get in a position so that I can act. The means that I use are secondary and they are not really related to my goal. If I can just play it right, I will land in a strategic position, maybe I will become the Governor of Palestine, and once I am Governor, there is a lot of autonomous authority that I will have and I can do all kinds of things for my fellow Jews, without my superiors ever knowing anything about it.

This is the way the structure is.

So the Tempter said:

— Yes, you can do that. But if you do it that way, it means one thing and one thing only — you must give up the initiative over your own life.

This is the heart of the dilemma.

What kind of advantage is of such significance to you or to me that in order to get it we will give up the moral initiative over our own lives? You have a job, and on it you are asked to do certain things that do violence to your own deep, central sense of integrity. But you need the job, and your children need to be fed; your wife needs medical attention; what difference, after all, does it make what I do? I am just one little man and the order of life is not affected by this. Who cares, anyway, about the little spot that I occupy? Should I ever give up the initiative over my own life? This is the dilemma. Even to save my life? What do you think?

Jesus resolved the dilemma by saying that man's central loyalty must always be to God and anything that conflicts with that is against God. If it is against God, it is against life, and if it is against life, it cannot abide. The first thing that is lost is a man's own soul. Do you believe that?

Think about this week that has just passed, or this month. For what kind of advantage did you give up the moral initiative over your own life? Was it worth it? What do you say to God when he asks you for an accounting? Do you say, I was in a tight place. I was afraid of pain. I am so temperamentally constituted that I cannot stand the rejection of my fellows. I want people to like me because this has been one of my problems all my life, feeling as if I was just a little on the outside and now this is a chance for me to get on the inside. To what have you said "yes," when as you said it, you felt the death pangs of something in you that was giving up the ghost? It was because Jesus was not willing to give up the initiative over his own life, even for a chance to get his hands on enough power that conceivably could alter the arrangement of affairs that they killed him. And he discovered that for a man who is willing to hold the initiative over his own life under God, even death is a little thing. Somehow he can stand whatever life does to him. This is not speculation. This is discovery.

Where do you stand? Where?

Lead us, O God, into paths from which our spirits shrink because the demand is so great. Give to us the quiet confidence, without trumpet blast, without arrogance and pride, declamation, flag waving, but just a simple, simple trust. Let us be true to that which Thou hast entrusted into our keeping, the integrity of our own souls. For us, O God, this is enough.

Amen.

At the Crossroad

Meditation:

We were delivered from something that threatened, something that would have destroyed or hurt or injured us, and we give to Thee the after-praise of our hearts, generated by the memory that survives. When we are most ourselves, we are concerned about doing the things which not only seem to our minds to be right and true, genuine and authentic, but which bring into our whole being a sense of peace, a sense of health and oneness.

We are troubled, our Father, by the divisions that are within us, deep conflicts in our own spirits which cause us to be at war within, a house divided against itself. This sense of inner conflict and the divisiveness is a part, as we think sometimes, our Father, of the conflict and the divisiveness that exists among Thy children everywhere. The peace which we seek in our private lives, that we may be one, is a part of the peace that we seek for all Thy children that they may be one family in Thy Presence, living in Thy world. How do we do this? If we only knew how to experience this, O God, with all our being. Out of Thy long experience with the life which Thou has created, the ups and downs of the journey of life by which Thou hast sought to make beauty out of ugliness, and harmony out of disharmony, wholeness out of things that are deep in their division, hast Thou learned so much that the overflow of Thy wisdom might be shared by us? May we too know how to win beauty out of ugliness, peace out of confusion, order out of chaos?

O God, how precious are Thy thoughts to us. How great is the sum of them.

Search me, O God, and know my heart. Try me and know my thoughts, and see if there be any wicked way in me. And lead me in the way everlasting. [47]

Temptations of Jesus

We continue our thinking together about the dilemmas of Jesus; this morning, the dilemma of the crossroad. As a background for our thought, I am reading two paragraphs from Olive Schreiner's *From Man to Man*.

"I have sometimes thought, it would be a terrible thing if, when death came to a man or a woman, there stood about his bed, reproaching him, not for his sins, not for his crimes of commission and omission toward his fellowmen, but for the thoughts and the visions that had come to him, and which he . . . had thrust always into the background. . . . And then, when he is dying, they gather round him, the things he might have incarnated and given life to—and would not. All that might have lived, and now must never live forever, look at him with their large reproachful eyes—his own dead visions reproaching him; . . . saying, 'We came to you; you, only you could have given us life. Now we are dead forever. Was it worth it? All the sense of duty you satisfied, the sense of necessity you labored under: should you not have violated it all and given us birth?' It has come upon me so vividly sometimes, that I have almost leaped out of bed to gain air—that suffocating sense that all his life long a man or a woman might live striving to do his duty and then at the end find it all wrong."

"There are such absolutely conflicting ideals; the ideal of absolute submission and endurance of wrong towards oneself—the ideal of noble resistance to all injustice and wrong, even when done to oneself—the ideal of the absolute devotion to the smaller, always present, call of life—and the ideal of a devotion to the larger aims sweeping all before it. . . . The agony of life is not the choice between good and evil, but between two evils or two goods!"

One of the common errors, to begin on a negative note, that we experience when we think reflectively about the meaning of the life of Jesus, is to isolate a particular event, and regard it as some-

[49]

thing which stands by itself alone, not a part of the process, the story, the living stuff of his career. For instance, on Good Friday all of the concentration of the mind and the thinking is on the crucifixion, as if his life began there, as if there were no birth, no development, no logic. And so it is with the temptations. We think of them as taking place in a moment in time. Once they have been dealt with, once he has conquered them, then he goes on triumphing in the light of this conquest. How unlike our lives this is. Every battle that you win, you must win over and over again, for as long as you are living and growing and experiencing and developing. This is dramatized in the dilemma of the crossroad. Let's get a feeling of the picture.

Jesus and his disciples had been in Jericho and as they were walking together on the road that leads out of Jericho, they approached the fork. One road went north to Galilee and Nazareth; the other went south to Jerusalem. As they neared, something strange apparently took place in Jesus' face and his whole body. He strode ahead of his disciples and when they looked in his face, they were frightened. This is the only place in the Gospels in which it is written that when the disciples looked into the face of the Master, they were frightened. They were frightened by what they saw in his face as he moved ahead of them and then made the sharp turn south—to Jerusalem.

Now what was going on in his mind? I don't know. I wasn't there. But I think that any reading of his life would indicate that this was one of the critical moments when he had to say, all over again, what he had said many times, as dramatized in the temptations. He had to decide again:

—What shall I do with my own life if I am to be true to the thing that sent me forth when I had the moment, unlike all other moments in any man's life, when he gathers together all the powers of his being and his mind and his personality and makes a decision. If he feels that the decision which he has made has the sanction of the God whom he worships, then he and his decision and his life, in that creative moment of swirling intensity become one thing. So, shall I go north? Back home? I have had a very interesting experience, a very meaningful experience. I have made several dry runs with reference to the insights of the Kingdom of God. I have had moments when it seemed to me I stood in that place where the old and the new and the future come together. I was on a Mount of Transfiguration once, and there my whole life was caught up in a movement which I recognized so fully and graphically all that the heart of Israel has been saying through Moses and all that the heart of Israel has been saying through the prophets came together for me in a moment of profound and intimate awareness. It was so vivid that I was sure that before my eyes stood Moses and the Prophets, and I shuddered with ineffable joy. I have touched with wholeness emotions that were wild and unstructured, and I have held such wholeness before wavering, distracted, tortured spirits until they knew what it meant to become domesticated, to become living instruments in the hands of a whole mind and a whole spirit. I have felt power moving through me as it touched and healed and helped; all this before my very eyes. I looked at the sick and as their agony broke my heart, I stormed the gates of heaven seeking one little increment of verity that I could transmit, if I could find in them any receptacle of faith and outreach. I have seen this; I have felt it. If I go back home now, I can live in the place with which I am familiar, and from all the ends of the region these people could come and be blessed and helped. What a comfort I would be to my mother who finds it so difficult to accept the fact that her oldest son has walked out from under the responsibilities left when the head of the family died. All this is the will of God, isn't it?

Perhaps, in the back of his mind, there was this thought:

—If I go home, then I can die in my bed. And how long I could live doing good, helping, teaching. The world needs somebody to teach it. If I could have a long time interval to make available to all who seek, that which moves in me, of which I am so fully conscious and aware, isn't this enough? What is wrong with that?

> So runs my dream. But what am I?
> An infant crying in the night;
> An infant crying for the light
> With no language but a cry . . .

This would be wonderful. . . . but I can't do it. I can't do it. I must go to Jerusalem. And I know that if I go to Jerusalem, the possibilities are I won't come back.

By making a choice to go to Jerusalem, am I simply following some egocentric impulse, some desire that has crept into my being that I thought I had conquered some time ago? I was convinced that even though I felt myself to be the living embodiment of the Kingdom of God, He would not make an exception in my case. If I go to Jerusalem, the possibility is that I may be mistaken about this. It may be true, you see, that if I go to Jerusalem God will just make it possible for me to get there, to teach, to take the position which is the logic of my commitment at a time when my act would be a defiance of religious and political authority. It would be something that I would have to do in order that the truth might be proclaimed.

It may be that I missed the reading when I was tempted to go up to the pinnacle of the temple and jump down. If I did, God would take care of me because he couldn't afford to run the risk of letting anything happen to me! Too much destiny rides on my continuing. And He knows that, so he will give his angels charge over me. They will bear me up and keep me from fulfilling the natural logic of my experience. Maybe the conclusion I reached was not right.

It is so difficult to find a way by which we may be protected from self-deception. I may be absolutely sure, now, but suppose I am wrong. How can I know whether I am right or not? Now, before I take the step into the future—if I could know, then everything else would be all right.

—Perhaps I misread it, and if I go to Jerusalem, maybe I am going just to prove that I was mistaken when I decided that life would *not* make an exception in my case.

He made his decision, and even though (and I say this with reverence) it was Jesus of Nazareth, even though it was Jesus Christ, in the decision that he made, he could have been mistaken. If he could not have been mistaken, there is no significance in the idea of a decision in the first place. This is the thing that ties his life to mine with hoops of steel! He gathered all the distilled wisdom, insight, brooding, devotion, worship, prayer and dedication of which he was capable, and standing within the movement of this kind of searching conviction, he acted, confident that in his act he would be sustained not merely as Jesus Christ, or not merely as Jesus of Nazareth. The insight of which he became the living embodiment was that this is the kind of world in which God would sustain and support and hold that insight that it might hold in his world. When? Five years from now? Six years? Twenty? A thousand? All of this has no particular significance. If I act within that kind of vivid religious experience—what is death, persecution, rejection? They have no significance.

—I must be careful now, lest when they come upon me, I make them significant. I must watch this, because the issue is not there! The issue is at another point. As long as I abide in it, if I live six weeks, six days, ten weeks, ten years, it doesn't make any difference. And I will not regard myself as a martyr, either. I will not say because I took this stand, or this position, and all the world came down upon me, won't somebody please come and help me out? Or, what were you doing that you let this happen to me?

These are all good thoughts, but irrelevant ones. Jesus did what he had to do! He moved out of the center which he held and which held him. I wish I could have been there. I wish I could have seen his eyes when he took the first step on the Jerusalem Road. It would have been worth a lifetime of living, just to feel the pull of that moment.

—Back home, and die in my bed. Go to Jerusalem; die on a hill.

When you face that kind of crossroad, as every human being does, how will you vote? As you have faced that kind of crossroad,

[53]

as every human being has, how did you vote? The answer is the story of your life.

> Lead us not into temptation, but deliver us from evil,
> For Thine is the Kingdom and the Power and the Glory
> Forever and ever.   Amen.

In the Garden

Temptations of Jesus

As a background for our discussion of the dilemma in the Garden
will you listen to this about Judas:

> The day I was born, so my mother says,
> The sun could not be seen from dawn to dusk
> The clouds tipped all the trees with gloom,
> The old folks shook their heads
> "It's a bad sign," they said.
>
> Years before I met the Master
> I saw his eyes in all my dreams.
> Face to face we met on the dusty road—
> He spoke: my heart replied.
> The pent up hunger of my restless years
> Poured forth, bringing the clean limpid feeling
> Of pure relief.
> We understood without the aid of speech
> The others talked their thoughts
> But between us only the muted, the crackling silence.
> Sometimes he seemed remote and far away
> Sometimes as close as air I breathed.
> Awareness would not let us go.
>
> At last, Jerusalem and the Temple!
> I remember his eyes,
> The frightened doves, the overturned tables
> The outraged cries.
> My heart rejoiced! The end was near
> For vaunting Roman and apostate Jew.
> That night while others slept, we talked
> We matched the secrets of our hearts.
> Like light appearing in a darkened room
> I knew!

How could I have been so blind?
I felt betrayed, outraged, uprooted from my place—
I fought with the only sword my hand could reach,
Not for him, not for my own poor self,
But for God's own holy Cause—
He was the Enemy—no Messiah he. . . .
Now it is done—
And I am alone, bereft—
What I have lost in life
In death may I find again?

The dilemma in the Garden is the facing of the same central problem, the same central temptation that did not ever quite desert the Master. He must fulfill the Word in him. And the Word was this: All of the children of men are children of God. The Word was the living embodiment of a way of living together that would confirm, in the stuff of life, the deep searching insistent intent of God, his Father. The dream did not stop there. How could this be done?

There is a way by which this dream, this intent, can become not merely literal truth but literal fact. In Jesus, the Kingdom was literal Truth, and the step from literal Truth to literal Fact involved implementation. To implement it men must ready themselves with moods, attitudes, feeling tones, desires, all summarized by the word Love.

But men can't do this by themselves, the dream continues. Because the dream is a part of the very intent of God, the resources of God are available on behalf of the translation of the dream from literal Truth to literal Fact. Over and over again Jesus said, "O men, how little you trust Him."

As this dream began to work, in all of its manifestations, it created tensions and pressures in the midst of a society that had not made up its mind. It is important for me to remember as I reflect upon this (and this may not be right, but it seems to me to be right) that there wasn't anything personal in this. The people who felt themselves threatened by this insistence on the part of the Master did not regard it as something that was personal and private, something that was focused or aimed at them in particular, but Jesus symbolized that which challenged and threatened the established structure. And the structure fought back, not merely because it did not like Jesus. That was not the point. The structure fought back because the structure did not want to be upset.

It is like the old fable of the frog and the yeastcake seated on the park bench. Someone dropped some water on the yeastcake, and it began fermenting and fermenting; expanding and expanding. The more it expanded, the more it crowded the frog. Finally, in desperation, the frog said, "Yeastcake, why don't you stop pushing me off the bench?" And the yeastcake said, "I'm not pushing you. I'm just growing."

Going back to "The *Temptation* in the Wilderness," this is the problem that faced the Master.

—Is there some other way? If I did a dramatic stunt, maybe that would do it. There must be some other way. I have tried to be careful in my commitment. I have not deliberately stirred up trouble. My aim has been sure and direct. I have not been a coward. I have not been afraid.

Even at the end, according to the record, every night the little band of disciples could be seen at sunset going out of the city, not merely because the city was perhaps crowded, but because they were in hiding. My own private feeling is that Jesus and his knot of disciples did not want to run any kind of risk of assassination in the darkness, so that Jesus would not be eliminated without the insistence of his whole life being faced—head-on! Men would have to make a clear choice, not a muted, fuzzy-edged one. Thus every night they were in hiding, and this is a part of the drama of the betrayal.

—How will we know him in the dark?

—I will kiss him, and you can pick him out.

He comes to the garden, still asking the same question. Is there some other way? He drops to his knees and begins to pray, stirring up from the bowels of life the cry, "Let the cup pass. Let the cup pass." There must be some other way!

I think it was there that Jesus wrestled with the problem of death. I think that when he got to the cross and was dying, the problem of death had been settled with him.

What is there about death that is so relevant here, and so relevant in the lives of any committed persons? Death as a literal act or experience in man's life is a denial of the future. I think this is why the human spirit shrinks from it; not merely because of the psychological and emotional overtones, the sense of loss—all of this is important, but it is on the edge. As long as there is an experience in the life of man that denies the future, this short-circuits the possibility of the meaning of the life and undercuts the grounds by which the interpretations of the significance of the past and the present find fulfillment. A way must be found to deal with this.

I can imagine him saying over again:

—Just a little time I've had. So many possibilities I see now. If I could work a little longer doing this or that or the other.... If I had time, (and this was the heart of the problem just outside of Jericho). If I had time. I need time.

It is not merely that at his age, he didn't want to die. That's perfectly natural, isn't it? There is nothing unusual about that. But to die with such a sense of 'my work not done.' And if I can convince myself that no one else can do the work, then death is a terror. This is the subtlety of the spiritual paradox that gripped his soul: The deeper the sense of commitment, the deeper the sense of full-orbed destiny that rode through all the reaches of his mind; the deeper his concentration, the more crucial his life seemed to be

[60]

for the fulfillment of the Kingdom of God. There must be some error here.

And then, with a thousand years between the two parts of the prayer, we hear him say:

—Nevertheless, it's your Kingdom, Father, not mine. And I trust you. I trust you. Even though I do not see, from where I am here prostrate, how You will do it, even though I do not now have room in me for a clue as to what You will do in order that that which is literal Truth in me will become literal Fact in all of the time-space involvements of Thy children, nevertheless, I trust You. Thy Will be done.

And thus the dilemma broke.

This is so hard, isn't it? I think that here Jesus is dealing with the most difficult thing in religious commitment: To be able to give up the initiative over your own life; to yield at the core of one's self, the nerve center of one's consent to God; and to trust the act itself.

We do not know His mind. We cannot fathom the mystery of God. We cannot even understand the meaning of our own little lives, but the fierce hold that we have on our lives, again and again, is the most real thing that we have. To relax that and to trust God—not to run His world, not to people His Universe, not to hold things in some kind of all-encompassing grasp; no, but to trust God just with you, with me, to say, "It's all right; my times are in Thy Hands"—is the most difficult dimension of the spiritual life. It was the experience of the Master, I think after trying and doing it here and there a little, that when he finally made the supreme and transcendent discovery that when a man is sure of God in that way, he can stand anything that life can do to him, and even death becomes a little thing.

When I contemplate his life and see all the little anxieties and misgivings that I have, I am astounded, confounded by what he did. I search the depths of my own soul to see if I may find some kind of clue from him that will help me do the same thing, and be answered. It may not matter whether any prayer any time was ever answered. If I am not answered, then all the answered prayers in the world are but confusing and confounding and distorting.

> "Heir of the Kingdom 'neath the skies
> Often he falls, yet falls to rise
> Stumbling, bleeding, beaten back
> Holding still to the upward track
> Playing his part in creation's plan
> Godlike in image—this is man."

The words rise and fall; the thoughts wax and wane, and always, Our Father, Thou dost hold us. Make us sense Thy strength in us. Help us to feel Thy trust in us. May we be reminded in all the ways that Thy vast creativity can conjure that Thou dost love us. Help us, O God, as we learn to love Thee.

To love Thee is the be all and end all of our living, Our Father.

Amen.